W9-CKB-476

ELEANOR ROOSEVELT
FIRST LADY OF THE WORLD

About the WOMEN OF OUR TIME™ Series

Today more than ever, children need role models whose lives can give them the inspiration and guidance to cope with a changing world. *WOMEN OF OUR TIME,* a series of biographies focusing on the lives of twentieth-century women, is the first such series designed specifically for the 7–11 age group. International in scope, these biographies cover a wide range of personalities—from historical figures to today's headliners—in such diverse fields as politics, the arts and sciences, athletics, and entertainment. Outstanding authors and illustrators present their subjects in a vividly anecdotal style, emphasizing the childhood and youth of each woman. More than a history lesson, the *WOMEN OF OUR TIME* books offer carefully documented life stories that will inform, entertain, and inspire the young people of our time.

Also in the WOMEN OF OUR TIME Series

BABE DIDRIKSON: Athlete of the Century
by R. R. Knudson

DOROTHEA LANGE: Life Through the Camera
by Milton Meltzer

DIANA ROSS: Star Supreme
by James Haskins

ELEANOR ROOSEVELT
FIRST LADY OF THE WORLD

BY DORIS FABER

Illustrated by Donna Ruff

VIKING KESTREL

VIKING KESTREL
Viking Penguin Inc., 40 West 23rd Street, New York, New York 10010, U.S.A.
Penguin Books Ltd, Harmondsworth, Middlesex, England
Penguin Books Australia Ltd, Ringwood, Victoria, Australia
Penguin Books Canada Limited, 2801 John Street, Markham, Ontario, Canada L3R 1B4
Penguin Books (N.Z.) Ltd, 182–190 Wairau Road, Auckland 10, New Zealand

First published in 1985 by Viking Penguin Inc.
Published simultaneously in Canada

"Women of Our Time" is a trademark of Viking Penguin Inc.

Library of Congress Cataloging in Publication Data
Faber, Doris,   Eleanor Roosevelt, first lady of the world.
Summary: A biography emphasizing the early years of Eleanor Roosevelt, who had
enormous political influence and won love and respect as America's first lady.
1. Roosevelt, Eleanor, 1884–1962—Juvenile literature.   2. Presidents—United States—
Wives—Biography—Juvenile literature.   [1. Roosevelt, Eleanor, 1884–1962.
2. First ladies]   I. Ruff, Donna, ill.   II. Title.
E806.1.R66F32   1985   973.917'092'4 [B] [92]   84-20861
ISBN 0-670-80551-3

Printed in the United States of America by The Book Press, Brattleboro, Vermont
1   2   3   4   5   89   88   87   86   85
Set in Garamond No. 3.

CONTENTS

ELEANOR ROOSEVELT
FIRST LADY OF THE WORLD

1

Father and Daughter

It was one of the first things she could remember.

All around her, wild confusion swirled. Grown people kept screaming. Suddenly, she felt herself being lifted up, then tossed a huge distance—down to where her father stood in a bobbing little boat, his arms raised.

Oh, how she clung to him after he caught her!

Eleanor Roosevelt was just two and a half when she had this terrifying experience of escaping from a sinking ship. Her parents were taking her on a trip to Europe, and their steamer had been hit by another

3

vessel during foggy weather. Happily, though, the second ship was hardly damaged, so it soon rescued everyone in the lifeboats.

But Eleanor never forgot her fear. From then on, she was very much afraid of boats and swimming. Also, she worried whenever her parents were out of her sight. No matter that in many ways she seemed very fortunate, she really had an unusually troubled childhood.

Anna Eleanor Roosevelt was her full name, and she had been born—on October 11, 1884—into the most privileged top layer of New York City's wealthy families. Both of her parents could trace ancestors back to the early days of America's founding.

Her mother, the former Miss Anna Hall, was a noted beauty. Eleanor's father, Elliott Roosevelt, called "Nell," was dashing, handsome, and lovable. But he had an extremely serious problem. He drank too much.

No doubt, part of the reason was a deep sense of despair. For Nell could not help comparing himself with his older brother, Theodore, who had gone into politics. In Teddy's own words, he was "rising like a rocket," while Nell just drifted—and drank.

Yet people in Nell's era believed in hiding unpleasant problems, especially from children. So Eleanor had no hint about what was wrong with her father. Once he took her for a walk and left her at the door-

4

way of a private club while he darted inside just for a few minutes, he said. Several hours later, she saw him carried out, senseless. Only then did a stranger notice the frightened child hovering nearby and take her home.

Eleanor loved her father so intensely, though, that his lapses did not matter to her. She adored him because he lavished love on her. He often called her his own darling "Little Nell."

Even after Eleanor's two younger brothers were born, she and her father continued this special closeness. She needed him desperately, because of the way her mother treated her. Although Mama was always kind to her, it was a cool and distant sort of kindness.

Eleanor tried very hard to earn more warmth. At the age of seven, she was already adept at gently stroking away the pain of Mama's frequent headaches. But Eleanor looked so solemn on such occasions that Mama greeted her oddly. "Come in, Granny," she would say. Eleanor hated this nickname, since she thought it explained why her mother did not love her.

Eleanor decided that she herself must be a particularly ugly child. Besides being much too tall, with a gawky way of walking, she knew she had awful front teeth. They stuck out so far that she often tried not to smile.

Still, she did not realize that she had beautiful eyes.

6

They were large and blue-gray, shining with her eagerness to please other people. As a result, most of her relatives considered her an exceptionally good and sweet little girl.

Soon after her seventh birthday, however, she suffered the first of a dreadful series of blows. Her father was taken away from her "to recover his health" while managing a horse farm in Virginia.

The following year, her mother became sick and died. Although Eleanor knew that she ought to feel sad, her first thought was: Now she could go and live with her father!

But Eleanor's mother had left instructions about the children's future. So Grandmother Hall took charge of Eleanor and her two brothers—and did all she could to discourage Elliott Roosevelt from seeing his children.

Eleanor cherished the scrawled letters he sent her from time to time. Every night she dreamed of being grown-up, when she and Father could be happy together. Even the grief she felt when her little brother, Elliott, died of diphtheria the next winter scarcely affected her dreams.

Then, shortly before she turned ten, she found out that her dreams would never come true. When she heard that her father, too, had died, she surprised her grandmother by taking the news so very quietly. After

7

a long silence, at last she spoke just a few heartbroken words.

"I did want to see him again."

2

A New Chance

During the next few years, Eleanor kept on imagining that, after all, she and her father were together. Absorbed by these daydreams, she managed to seem calm even though she felt dreadfully unhappy.

Of course, her life might have struck a lot of poor children as far from miserable. Eleanor's summers were spent at her grandmother's country mansion overlooking the Hudson River, and her winters in a grand townhouse near New York City's Madison Avenue. Besides numerous servants, there were always plenty of relatives around her.

Young aunts and uncles made both houses livelier. Aunt Maude was just six years older than Eleanor, and Aunt "Pussie" about ten years older, so they became something like her big sisters.

"Totty," they called her, being fond of nicknames. To them it meant she was a likable tot, and yet they were often too busy to pay much attention to her. So was Grandmother Hall, a well-meaning but not very loving widow. As Eleanor entered her teens—growing taller than any other girl at the private school she attended—her inner despair grew, too.

She thought most people pitied her because she was an orphan and because of her "plain" appearance. So Eleanor could not help envying other girls who had been born pretty.

Still, she hid the way she felt because she knew her father would have wished it. She even stopped biting her fingernails when she decided that her father would have frowned on that weakness. Also, she patiently read poetry aloud to Aunt Pussie, and she tried to be a substitute mother for her brother Hall, seven years younger.

As a result, Eleanor rarely had any lighthearted fun. Almost her only opportunities came when Grandmother Hall allowed her to visit her Roosevelt relatives on Long Island. Vacationing at Oyster Bay, Uncle Ted was always bursting with high spirits. He would

10

have his own children and any visiting nieces or nephews join hands, then run down a sandy hill right into the water. Although the idea terrified Eleanor, she forgot to be afraid amid so much laughter.

It pleased her tremendously that Uncle Ted congratulated her for being a good sport. Her brave efforts to conquer her fears and her clumsiness at games delighted him. He even told her she was his favorite niece.

But Eleanor's grandmother let her go to Oyster Bay only occasionally. Mrs. Hall did give her a far more important chance, though, in 1899—when she was fifteen. Eleanor was sent then to a select boarding school three thousand miles away, in England.

Right from her first days there, Eleanor was happy at Allenswood. Wearing the school uniform of a white blouse and a long black skirt, taking daily walks in any sort of weather, keeping her own belongings tidy— all of this made sense to her. And she liked being part of a group, no longer an outsider.

Since no one knew her sad history, she did not have to worry about being pitied by her new classmates. Nor did her plain appearance cause any headshaking. At Allenswood, excelling in the classroom was considered more important.

When Eleanor quickly showed that she had a keen mind as well as a sympathetic nature, she won both

respect and affection. She also convinced a remarkable teacher that here was a pupil worthy of special attention.

Although most of the forty girls at Allenswood were English, the school was run by a white-haired woman from France—Mademoiselle Marie Souvestre. "Sou," as the students called her privately, had a lively interest in everything under the sun, including politics and other topics not supposed to concern females then. "Why was your mind given you but to think things out for yourself?" she would ask.

This unusual woman devoted many evenings to expanding Eleanor's mental horizons by discussing current events with her. During school vacations, she took her on wide-ranging sightseeing trips to France and Italy. And Eleanor amply repaid her teacher's faith in her.

By the autumn of 1901—in the same month that Theodore Roosevelt became the twenty-sixth president of the United States—his nearly seventeen-year-old niece had earned a high rank of her own. At every meal in the Allenswood dining room, Eleanor took the seat directly opposite Mademoiselle Souvestre. It was the place of honor, reserved for the top student in this outstanding school.

3

Cousin Franklin

Eleanor was nearing her eighteenth birthday when she returned to America. She felt very different from the hopeless girl who had departed three years earlier. And she even looked different.

With her new air of self-confidence, she no longer made her aunts murmur to each other about how gawky the poor child was. True, she had grown much too tall—five feet and a full ten inches. And, oh, those dreadful front teeth still protruded terribly!

Yet her slender figure was attractive in the Paris frocks she had brought back. Her light-brown hair, pinned in a soft upsweep, shone like silk. Also, those blue-gray eyes of hers radiated such an alert interest and sympathy upon anyone she was talking to that she did seem almost pretty. Yes, the aunts concluded, dear Eleanor might do quite well, after all.

Under her serene manner, however, Eleanor had buried a new fear.

Among families like hers, it was the custom for every young woman to "come out" the year she turned eighteen. This meant attending dozens of formal parties, large and small, introducing her to New York society. But the real goal was to give her a chance to charm some suitable young man into seeking her as his wife.

Eleanor dreaded the whole experience, because she was sure no young man would ask her to dance, let alone marry him. It happened, though, that one day in the early autumn, on a train going up to the country, she encountered someone who took her mind off the test ahead of her.

It was her cousin Franklin. He was a fifth cousin, who belonged to a separate branch of the Roosevelt family. The two young people hardly knew each other, but she could remember being taken, when she was very young, to visit Franklin and his parents in Hyde Park, not far from Grandmother Hall's country house. What Eleanor recalled, actually, was being bounced about, piggyback-style, on the back of this boy cousin two years older than she was.

Now Franklin was twenty, a Harvard student—and unbelievably handsome. At least six feet tall, not a bit shy, he greeted Eleanor with a warm smile.

Over the next year, Cousin Franklin increasingly sought Eleanor's company. His frequent visits to New York kept her from suffering nearly as much as she had feared during the process of coming out. And it surely did not seem as if he was paying her all of this attention just because he pitied her.

He appeared, instead, to enjoy conversing with her on serious topics. A few afternoons a week, she served as a volunteer teacher in a school in a slum neighborhood, and Franklin, unlike most people in their circle, wanted to hear about the unpleasant sights she saw there.

One afternoon, Franklin came to call for Eleanor at the school, and a little girl asked them to walk her home. Leaving the filthy and foul-smelling building where the child lived, Franklin clapped a hand to his brow. He never knew that human beings had to live in such places, he said.

So Eleanor supposed that she might be helping her cousin learn some things he was not taught at Harvard. If he went in for politics, as he told her he wanted to, she thought that perhaps such knowledge might help him.

16

Then, when she was visiting Boston on a weekend shortly after her nineteenth birthday, Franklin astounded her—by asking her to marry him.

In her confusion, Eleanor stammered a question of her own. Why me? she asked. For she was plain, and he could have any pretty girl he wanted.

But he wanted *her,* Franklin insisted. With her at his side, there was no limit to what he could accomplish. Besides, he happened to be very much in love with her. So Eleanor finally allowed herself to admit that she, too, had fallen in love.

An extremely strong obstacle remained to be conquered, though. Franklin's mother, a rich widow, had a will of iron. Sara Delano Roosevelt doted on her only son, and she protested that "the dear children" were far too young to think of marrying.

Franklin never fought with his mother, but he found other ways to do as he wished. While Eleanor nervously tried to make "Cousin Sally" like her, he figured out a compromise. He agreed to wait a year before telling anyone else he and Eleanor were engaged, provided that his mother gave her consent when the year ended.

It was a difficult year, but it went faster than Eleanor expected. Finally, she and Franklin could reveal the secret they had been keeping.

Then came a flood of good wishes, along with a

18

warmhearted offer from the President of the United Sates. Would they like their wedding held at the White House? For Uncle Ted said he was as fond of Eleanor as if she were his own daughter.

Eleanor worried, though, that the White House would be too much like a fishbowl. So arrangements were made to have the ceremony at the home of a wealthy New York cousin. Still, the date was set to suit Uncle Ted. It was March 17, 1905—St. Patrick's Day—when he would be coming to New York anyway, to review the parade there.

Because of Uncle Ted's presence, police lined the street outside the stone mansion where the wedding took place. Inside, the twenty-year-old bride, tall and solemn and amazingly beautiful in white satin, walked slowly forward, escorted by her uncle. At the front of the room, a canopy of pink roses hung above an altar. Beside it, the handsome groom waited.

The instant the service was over, the President kissed his niece. "Well, Franklin," Uncle Ted cried, "there's nothing like keeping the name in the family!" Then he bounded off toward the refreshment table.

Mr. and Mrs. Franklin Delano Roosevelt stood where they were, expecting to be surrounded by well-wishers. Instead, almost all the guests moved in the opposite direction—to hear what the president might say next.

Franklin seemed a bit dismayed. But soon he began to joke about the way Uncle Ted was "stealing the show." After just a few minutes, the young couple joined the crowd around their famous relative.

4

Babies, Just Babies

Eleanor and Franklin spent the next few months very happily in a hotel near Columbia University, where he had started to study law. "Dearest Honey," she called him when they were alone together, and, for some private reason, he called her "my darling Babs." That summer, they had a delightful honeymoon, touring much of Europe.

By the time they got back to New York, Eleanor was on her way toward becoming a mother. Many years later she would recall with a touch of humor that, during the first ten years of her married life, she

22

was always either expecting a baby or getting over just having had a baby. It was nearly true.

In May 1906, she gave birth to a daughter they named Anna. In December of the following year, James arrived. Both were beautiful, healthy infants, good-natured and fond of being the center of attention.

So was Franklin Junior, born in March 1909. But this newest addition to the family proved to be less sturdy than he looked, and at the age of seven months, he developed an acute illness. He died the next day.

Eleanor mourned intensely, and she even blamed herself for the tragedy, although doctors told her nothing could have saved the baby. Her depression lifted only gradually after she had another son, the quick-tempered but lovable Elliott, born in September 1910.

Two more sons were still to come. Enough time had elapsed by 1914 for another boy to be named Franklin Junior. Then, two years later, lively and mischievous Frankie was joined by John.

During these ten years of childbearing, Eleanor tried hard to be a model wife and mother. She even quit her volunteer teaching, to make sure she would not bring home any germs that might infect her own children.

Yet she often felt as if she herself hardly existed. Not that the care of her five active "chicks" over-

whelmed her, for she had plenty of servants to help her. But someone else hired them.

It was Franklin's mother. As a wedding present, the elder Mrs. Roosevelt had not only given her son and his wife a new house, but also she had furnished it to her own taste. Then she moved right next door on Manhattan's stylish East Sixty-fifth Street.

At first, Eleanor meekly accepted advice from "Mama" because of her own inexperience. Mama, of course, had positive opinions on every subject. "Don't say your hands are 'dirty,' " she would tell a grandson. "The proper word is 'soiled.' "

Over the years, however, Eleanor grew increasingly distressed by Mama's interference. Still, her sense of duty forced her to keep silent. She did not dare object even when Mama hired a strict nursemaid the children nicknamed "Old Battle-Ax."

One day this woman punished the oldest Roosevelt son in a very cruel way. Jimmy had told her he already had brushed his teeth but she did not believe him. She made him dress in his sister's skirt, then pinned a sign on his back. I AM A LIAR, it said.

When Eleanor returned from a shopping trip, she saw Jimmy miserably parading up and down the city sidewalk in front of their house, while passing strangers stared at him. Her eyes filled with tears, and she hurried her son inside. Still, she was afraid to fire Old Battle-Ax. What would Mama say then?

25

Instead, Eleanor kept a close watch over the nurse, and soon she suspected something that made her search the woman's room. In it, she found several whiskey bottles.

Now Eleanor felt safe, because Mama shared her horror of drinking. So she ordered Old Battle-Ax to pack up and leave the house immediately. Then Eleanor all by herself hired a gentle woman from Scotland to watch over her children. This was her first small step toward declaring her independence.

Unlike Franklin, Eleanor could not merely laugh off the elder Mrs. Roosevelt's queenly ways. In fact, Franklin was altogether much more lighthearted than his young wife. Going to kiss "the chicks" good night, he would cheerfully ask each of them, "Are you snug as a bug in a rug?" Eleanor, nervously glancing at her gold watch, would always be in a hurry to bundle them off to sleep.

Yet Franklin proved—in 1910, when he was just twenty-eight—that he did have a serious side. That year, he ran for a seat in the New York State Senate. He ran as a Democrat, in a strongly Republican area, and he surprised a good many political observers by winning his first contest. He surprised his wife, too.

But politics hardly interested Eleanor at this period of her life. For her, Franklin's victory merely meant that she escaped daily outings with her mother-in-law.

26

Throughout three winters in Albany, Eleanor Roosevelt remained a homebody. Her main concern was protecting her children against the clouds of cigar smoke that wafted upstairs whenever Franklin's new friends came to visit him.

In these years, an increasing number of women around the country were marching in parades, holding up banners demanding the right to vote. But the young Mrs. Roosevelt thought then that only domestic duties should occupy her mind. Even so, politics had a great effect on her own life.

In 1912, her husband strongly supported Woodrow Wilson's bid to become president and, when Wilson won, Franklin Roosevelt's efforts were rewarded. This rich young man, who had always been fascinated by ships, was appointed as the principal aide to the new president's secretary of the Navy. So, in the spring of 1913, at the age of twenty-eight, Eleanor took up housekeeping in Washington.

As Mrs. Assistant Secretary of the Navy, she was expected to attend many formal dinner parties and to spend her afternoons paying calls on the wives of other officials. By now she felt less fearful about mingling with strangers, but official gatherings often bored or irritated her.

Yet Eleanor was still afraid to seek some more interesting occupation. Instead, she plunged into

27

proving what a diligent partygoer she could be. She even hired a pretty young woman to help her a few mornings a week with all the letter-writing required by such an active social life.

Then, in 1917, the United States was drawn into the war that had been raging in Europe for the last several years—the terrible conflict that afterward would be called the First World War. Mrs. Roosevelt's tireless energy finally found a satisfying outlet. Suddenly,

thousands of soldiers crammed every train passing through Washington's railroad station, and the Red Cross was asked to provide coffee and sandwiches for them. Soon a tall and purposeful woman emerged as the efficient director of this emergency program.

In a way, Eleanor's increasingly complicated household duties had prepared her to assume this job. It might seem that any woman with ten servants would have almost nothing to do at home herself. In fact,

Mrs. Roosevelt kept careful track of every penny the family spent. And she did so much organizing that she was like the commander-in-chief of a small army.

Several times every year she made all the plans for moving five children and ten servants from Washington to New York City or Hyde Park. She also directed a grand journey every summer up to the family's cottage on the island of Campobello, off the coast of Maine—for this vacation, at least seventy boxes and barrels and suitcases had to be packed.

Yet it was not until Eleanor's wartime service with the Red Cross that she realized what a competent person she was. Also, she realized for the first time how deeply she craved a chance to do some useful work. Then, shortly after the war ended in 1918, Mrs. Roosevelt found another reason why she *needed* work.

Unpacking Franklin's luggage on his return from a trip, she noticed some letters in a familiar handwriting. Her own pretty secretary, Lucy Mercer, had written them. A glance showed her that these were love letters.

To a woman like Eleanor Roosevelt, who had the strictest of moral standards, it was impossible just to forgive Franklin. But when he promised never to see Lucy again, Eleanor coldly said that, for the sake of their children, she would continue living with him.

As much as Franklin had hurt her, though, she

30

could not help blaming herself for what had happened. If she had been a better wife, she kept brooding, he never would have strayed. And it seemed to her that she simply could not go on day after day—unless she did some work that would make her stop feeling entirely useless.

5

"I hear them all laughing . . ."

During the autumn of 1920, Mrs. Roosevelt found herself having to smile at a lot of strangers—because she was the wife of the Democratic candidate for vice-president of the United States.

In that same year, an amendment to the Constitution finally gave the women of America the basic right to vote. So Eleanor Roosevelt, casting her first ballot, voted for the vice-presidential candidate who happened to be her husband.

The Democrats lost, though, and the Roosevelt family returned to New York City. While Franklin resumed practicing law, Eleanor joined the League of Women Voters. She spent many rewarding hours attending meetings or writing reports about laws of special interest to women. Then came a terrible new crisis.

Up at their summer cottage in Maine, Franklin returned from an afternoon sail saying that he felt awfully tired. Eleanor urged him to go right to bed and get a really good sleep. But the next morning Franklin could not move his legs.

At first, the local doctor reassured them. Merely a severe cold, he said. A few days of rest would cure it. Luckily, a gruff little man Eleanor had originally disliked was staying with them. Louis Howe, an Albany newspaper reporter who had quit his own writing to devote himself to helping Franklin's political career, insisted on getting another doctor from the mainland. The expert spoke a dreaded word.

Polio. Franklin, at the age of thirty-nine, had somehow caught the crippling disease that usually struck children. The doctor gave orders for round-the-clock nursing care, which Eleanor herself undertook. But neither she nor Louis dared to ask: Would Franklin ever walk again?

Instead, these two formed an instant plot to behave as cheerfully as possible, and Franklin bravely joined them. Even Franklin's mother dried her tears. "I hear

33

them all laughing," she wrote to her brother. "Eleanor in the lead." During the next few weeks, the elder Mrs. Roosevelt said she was trying to follow her daughter-in-law's "glorious example."

But Sara Delano Roosevelt soon decided that her son was bound to remain an invalid, and she wanted him safely at Hyde Park, sitting in a wheelchair, puttering with his collection of stamps.

No! Eleanor would not accept this future for the vigorous man she had married. While he kept doggedly working at a very painful program of exercise, she did more than just encourage him. For the first time in her married life, she dared to argue with her mother-in-law.

Eleanor also spoke up in another way. Because Louis Howe thought that Mrs. Franklin Delano Roosevelt could keep her husband's name from being forgotten, she forced herself to start making nervous little speeches at Democratic women's gatherings.

6

The Wife of the Governor

By 1928, seven years after Franklin's illness, he could stand up with heavy metal braces attached to both legs. He could even walk a few dozen steps, leaning on the strong arm of one of his sons.

And his wife was a leading figure in the women's division of the New York State Democratic Committee. Eleanor had learned to edit the division's monthly magazine. She also made many trips around the state to raise money or sign up new voters.

As if that were not enough to keep her busy, Mrs. Roosevelt was one of the owners of a private high school for girls, where she taught literature and current events a few days a week. She used her own notebooks from Allenswood as the basis for her lessons.

Nor had her own family ceased requiring attention. Anna, her daughter, had already married and produced an adorable granddaughter. Although the four Roosevelt sons were away, either at Harvard or boarding school, their antics or their health problems often made their mother drop everything else. But her main worry was her younger brother, Hall, whom she had always considered as her eldest son. It bothered her terribly to see Hall drinking too much, the way their father had.

All in all, though, the forty-four-year-old Mrs. Roosevelt felt satisfied, if not really happy. For she and Franklin had never come back to the closeness of their early married life. Part of her still wished it would happen, and she started her letters to him "Dearest Honey," when he went down to Warm Springs, Georgia several times every year. But she rarely went with him to the treatment center he had founded there for polio victims. By now, they each had their own friends and special interests.

Yet Eleanor was well aware that plans for Franklin to get into politics again constantly occupied him and Louis Howe. She herself was doing all she could to

36

help them. Even so, she shuddered inwardly when Franklin agreed, in September 1928, to run for governor of New York.

Duty, though, was a word she could not ignore. So Eleanor worked behind the scenes to organize get-out-the-vote drives among Democratic women. Her efforts may have made a crucial difference, for it was by the narrowest of margins that Franklin won the election.

Then Mrs. Roosevelt had to ask herself: Could she, somehow, fulfill the social duties of a governor's wife without giving up her own cherished freedom? Briskly, she set out trying the experiment.

Every Sunday evening, she left the Governor's Mansion in Albany with a briefcase under her arm. Wasting not a minute during her three-hour train ride down to New York City, she marked exam papers and prepared lessons for her classes. On Wednesday afternoon she returned to Albany for a hectic weekend as the hostess at official gatherings. It was a routine that would have exhausted most other people, but Eleanor Roosevelt thrived on it.

Now her tremendous curiosity overcame the fears of her girlhood. When she went to Lake Placid for the ceremonies opening the Winter Olympics there, she cheerfully accepted an invitation to try a ride down the bobsled run herself. It was a grand experience, she told her husband afterward. He laughed and said he supposed the next thing he heard would be that she'd gone up in some newfangled airplane. He was right.

In addition to having fun, though, she also felt useful. Every summer, she helped Franklin in a very important way on his trips around the state to inspect prisons, hospitals, and other institutions. Since he could not walk any distance, at every stop he sat in his car chatting about politics with local officials. Meanwhile, his wife strode through the buildings from basement to attic—she even lifted the lids of the pots on the kitchen stove to make sure nobody fooled her, or her husband, about what was cooking.

Mrs. Roosevelt's concern about the less fortunate increased after the Wall Street stock market crashed in 1929—and millions of Americans lost their jobs. It is very difficult, more than half a century later, to realize how much misery the Great Depression caused during the next several years. There was no unemployment insurance then, or any other government program for helping a vast number of people to endure unrelieved hardship.

By 1932, the situation was desperate. In this election year, the Democratic party picked as its candidate for president of the United States a man whose personal courage and jaunty smile—even more than his

ringing words about creating "a New Deal"—somehow inspired hope.

Eleanor Roosevelt still could not help dreading the prospect of becoming just the official hostess at the White House. But, along with the majority of her fellow citizens, she cast her ballot for Franklin Delano Roosevelt.

So it happened that, on March 4, 1933, this unusually thoughtful, energetic, and ungainly woman of forty-eight became the First Lady of the Land.

7

Mrs. R. Emerges

Less than a week later, an outstanding woman reporter in New York received a letter from her dearest friend. It was written on an elegant sheet of paper headed, in gold, THE WHITE HOUSE.

Beneath this, following a breathless account of comings and goings, Eleanor Roosevelt had scrawled a particularly notable sentence: "I begin to think there may be ways in which I can be useful."

To Lorena Hickok, who covered politics for the Associated Press, those words were not surprising. Ever since the presidential campaign had started, "Hick"

41

had felt sure that F.D.R.'s wife was an exceptional person, and the two women had become close friends.

But it was not until Eleanor Roosevelt settled into the White House that the whole country began to see what Hick had seen. Just as a small sign of her independence, the new First Lady rolled up her sleeves and moved some furniture herself—to make the White House living quarters seem more homey.

Soon she was dashing around Washington, inspecting the disgraceful slums right in the shadow of the Capitol or visiting the camp set up by hundreds of jobless ex-soldiers. All of this activity made lively stories in the newspapers. So did the weekly press conferences Mrs. Roosevelt started holding.

Because she wanted "to do something for women," only women reporters were admitted to these regular sessions. Naturally, the handful of female journalists in Washington marveled at the luck that had given them Mrs. R. Together, they created something new on the American scene.

Every previous First Lady had dealt with the press only indirectly, by having a social secretary who handed out bare lists of the guests invited to White House dinners or other gatherings. But now a warmhearted public figure with strong opinions of her own was emerging. And the women reporters gladly spread this news, telling the whole country Mrs. Roosevelt's

42

latest comments about serious subjects like international cooperation. Of course, they also wrote about the First Lady's quite unconsciously funny—and mistaken—idea that Franklin very much enjoyed economy meals, such as hard-boiled eggs in cream sauce and stewed prunes.

To friends like Hick, Mrs. Roosevelt continued wailing about the loss of her personal freedom. What she hated most, she said, was being stared at by mobs of people. She did not seem to notice, however, that this private distress almost ceased during her first few years as First Lady.

The inner change probably started as she sat up late, night after night, going over her mail. While it was not unusual for the wife of any president to receive appeals for help, or even praise from strangers, Washington had never seen anything like the avalanche of appeals and praise that soon descended on Eleanor Roosevelt.

Three hundred thousand letters, from everywhere in the country, were addressed to her in 1933 alone. Incredibly, she and her secretary, Malvina Thompson—the selfless "Tommy"—made sure that every letter received an answer, often containing specific advice. At last Eleanor felt not only really needed, but also really admired. Then, finally, she stopped *feeling* homely.

As a result, she no longer froze whenever a camera was aimed at her. Pictures of her began showing the warm smile or the expression of eager interest that only those who knew her well had ever been aware of before. A similar change in her voice could be heard when she was asked to "say a few words."

Instead of the nervous, high-pitched tone that radio comedians had taken to imitating, Mrs. Roosevelt spoke with ease in front of even the largest audiences after she stopped worrying about her appearance. And, in 1935, she started giving lectures all around the country. People, by the thousands, paid to hear her talk on topics like world peace or a typical day at the White House. These speaking tours were a great success, filling big auditoriums wherever she went.

But this lecturing made some people angry. The First Lady had no right using her position to make herself rich, they said. Mrs. Roosevelt brushed aside such criticism. Why shouldn't she earn money to help the worthy causes she would otherwise not be able to afford supporting?

Mrs. Roosevelt earned money writing, too. Along with numerous articles for magazines, she wrote a daily column, "My Day," printed in hundreds of newspapers from coast to coast.

On top of everything else, in 1936, when her husband was running for a second term and she had to

44

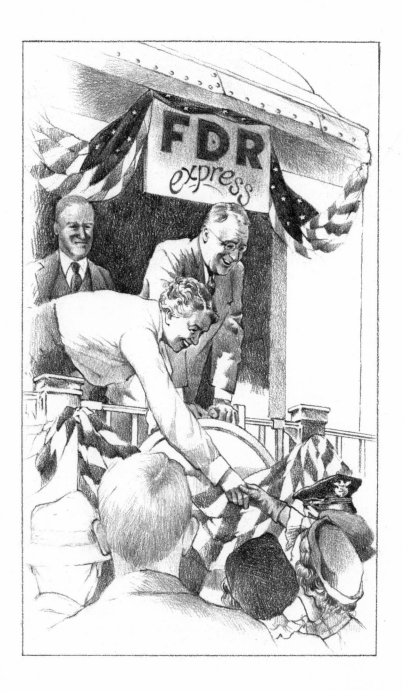

travel around the country with him aboard his campaign train, she used the time between each stop to write a book about her own early life. *This Is My Story,* she called it.

It became a best-seller! One of Mrs Roosevelt's new friends, the noted author Dorothy Canfield Fisher, tried to tell her why: "You see, I think you are a kind of genius. Out of your personality and position you have created something of unique value . . . an example."

8

"Gosh, there's Eleanor!"

Under ordinary circumstances, Eleanor Roosevelt would have stopped being the First Lady after the 1940 election. But another terrifying war had begun in Europe the preceding year, and it seemed that the United States might not be able to stay out of the conflict much longer. Because of this great danger, the Democrats chose Franklin Roosevelt as their candidate again—even though no other president had ever served more than two terms. Mrs. Roosevelt felt strongly that, for the sake of the nation, her husband should be reelected in November.

47

For her own sake, though, she still could not help wishing F.D.R. had decided to retire. By now, she hardly minded having strangers peer at her every place she went. In her cheeriest moods, she came right out and admitted that she enjoyed many of the advantages of her high position. But one aspect of her celebrity increasingly depressed her.

Mrs. Roosevelt thought that she could bear criticism as well as most people. At the White House, she once asked an Oyster Bay cousin to do her famous imitation of the First Lady—and the First Lady herself laughed with obvious good humor when Cousin Alice boldly obliged. But the amount of criticism, and the kind of criticism, aimed at Eleanor Roosevelt soon ceased to amuse her.

For, if no other First Lady had ever been as widely admired as Mrs. Roosevelt, the opposite was true, too. Some newspapers made her "do-good" efforts their favorite target, day after day. There were diehard Republicans who actually felt sorry for Franklin because he had such a busybody of a wife.

Still, the 1940 campaign proved that Mrs. Roosevelt had attained a rare standing. At the Democratic convention that nominated F.D.R. to run for an unprecedented third term, many delegates had very mixed feelings about defying a tradition that went back to the days of George Washington. They showed this by angrily booing Henry Wallace, F.D.R.'s own choice for vice-president.

To calm the ugly revolt, the Democratic chairman telephoned Hyde Park and made an urgent request. Would *Mrs. Roosevelt* please fly out to Chicago? Never before had the wife of a president addressed a political convention, but Franklin agreed that Eleanor should go.

As soon as the unruly delegates recognized Mrs. R. walking toward the front of the platform, they quieted. She spoke only a few minutes, like a kindly teacher who knew her class really wanted to do its best. At a time of national emergency, she said, any president deserved the help of every patriotic citizen. Surely, then, the delegates had a duty to make the President's job easier by giving him the running mate he preferred.

After Mrs. Roosevelt finished, there was utter silence. Then cheers erupted all over the huge auditorium—and the convention voted in an orderly way, without a single boo, to nominate the vice-president F.D.R. wanted.

On December 7, 1941, the Japanese attacked Pearl Harbor in Hawaii. By then, Mrs. Roosevelt had an actual job assisting the director of the nation's civilian defense program. She flew out to California the next day because of frightening rumors that enemy planes were about to bomb the West Coast.

"I seem to have a calming effect," she wrote to her old friend Hick.

On countless occasions already—in a coal mine, an auto factory, at the top of a mountain—someone had glanced up and seen a tall woman who looked familiar. Then came the cry: "Gosh, there's Eleanor!" During the war, American soldiers all over the world had the same experience.

50

The First Lady became the symbol of home to millions of homesick fighting men. Everywhere she went, she copied down the names and addresses of "the boys" she talked with, then wrote heartwarming notes to their parents on her return.

In these wartime years, her popularity soared, and much of the former criticism was forgotten. Yet it sometimes seemed to her that everybody appreciated her except her husband. Once she came hurrying into his study while he was relaxing before dinner, and she briskly handed him a sheaf of requests. The President

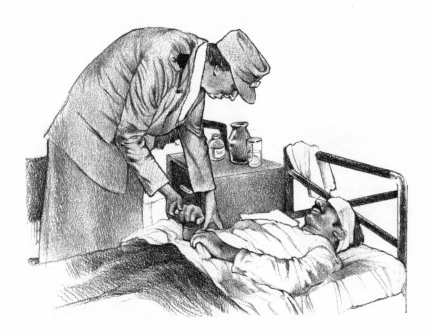

hurt her deeply then. He shook his head and tossed the papers toward their daughter, Anna, saying, "Here, Sis, *you* take care of these tomorrow."

Being tireless herself, Mrs. Roosevelt failed to sense how tired her husband was becoming. By the end of his third term, with the war in Europe nearly won, it seemed to her beyond question that he must run again so he could direct victory in the Pacific, too. In 1944, a weary and ailing F.D.R. did summon enough of his former fire to win another four years in the White House.

But on April 12, 1945, while he was resting in Warm Springs, Georgia, Franklin Roosevelt suddenly fainted. A few hours later, while his wife was making a speech in Washington, he died.

9

On Her Own

Outwardly calm, Mrs. Roosevelt waited at the White House for the Vice-President. In the last election, Senator Harry Truman of Missouri had been selected as F.D.R.'s running mate.

"Harry," Mrs. Roosevelt said gently, when he arrived, "the President is dead."

Truman's eyes filled with tears. His first words to Mrs. Roosevelt were, "Is there anything I can do for you?"

Mrs. Roosevelt replied as if her own feelings did not matter: "Is there anything *we* can do for you? For you are the one in trouble now."

Throughout the next few days, in Warm Springs and then aboard the slow train carrying a coffin draped with the American flag northward, past mourning thousands standing all along the track, Mrs. Roosevelt remained composed. Only she knew what emotions churned beneath her quiet dignity during the solemn funeral ceremonies in Washington and Hyde Park.

Then an unusually subdued Mrs. Roosevelt supervised the swift packing-up of personal possessions that had accumulated in the White House during her family's twelve years there. She said she would spend most of her time at her own cottage in Hyde Park, peacefully surrounded by grandchildren. She would be no leader of thought or action, she wrote to her old friend Hick. Now she would have plenty of time for reading, relaxing, perhaps even taking up gardening.

It did not happen.

In the autumn of 1945, soon after her sixty-first birthday, Mrs. Roosevelt received a telephone call from the White House. President Truman wanted to appoint her to represent the United States at the first meeting of the new United Nations in London. By now the war had ended—and how could she refuse? For she and Franklin both had been strongly convinced that only an effective international organization could guarantee a lasting peace.

Mrs. Roosevelt spent the rest of her life striving to

54

promote the cause of peace. "The First Lady of the World," President Truman would call her.

She retired from the U.N. when she was nearly seventy, but she still did not stop speaking and traveling. She went to Russia and Japan, to Israel and India, visiting peasants and prime ministers, always spreading the message that world peace depended on international friendship.

At home, Eleanor Roosevelt had more political influence than any other woman in American history. Would she have acquired such power if the man she married had not become an outstanding president?

Probably not. For Franklin Roosevelt had undoubtedly opened a great opportunity to her. But her own energy and amazing capacity to keep on learning surely were almost as significant. Fifteen years after F.D.R.'s death, his widow's word carried so much weight that a young man named John F. Kennedy came to seek her approval before he began campaigning for the presidency in 1960.

By then, Mrs. Roosevelt had begun failing. Yet she kept writing and speaking two more years—until a complicated blood disease made her enter a hospital. Shortly after her seventy-eighth birthday, on November 7, 1962, this world-famous woman died.

Her funeral in Hyde Park was attended by President Kennedy and also by two former presidents,

Truman and Eisenhower, as well as a future president, Lyndon Johnson. Yet a man who had twice lost to Eisenhower spoke the most moving words about Eleanor Roosevelt after her death.

"She would rather light a candle than curse the darkness," said Adlai Stevenson. "And her glow has warmed the world."

ABOUT THIS BOOK

Readers often ask three kinds of questions when they finish one of my books—questions that start with "How?" or "Where?" or "Why?"

First, *how* did I find the facts? Everything in this book about Eleanor Roosevelt is based on the memories of people who knew her, on her own words, or on other evidence preserved at the F.D.R. Library in Hyde Park.

And Hyde Park is also *where* any reader interested in Mrs. Roosevelt should try to go. Adjoining the library, about eighty miles north of New York City, is a museum with a separate wing devoted just to Eleanor Roosevelt. Hundreds of items on display range from her christening robe to the fascinating assortment of cards and scraps of verse found in her purse after she died.

Finally, *why* did I want to write about her? That goes back to my days as a young reporter for *The New York Times,* when I covered many meetings attended by the eminent Mrs. R. Around the time she moved on to the United Nations, I retired to raise two daughters—and write books. One was about her husband, another about her friend Lorena Hickok, but until now I have not had the pleasure of writing about Mrs. R. herself. 　　　D.F.

JB Roosevelt F 110686
Faber, Doris
Eleanor Roosevelt, first
lady of the world

9/05   17   3/03
6-16   19   3-16

1/20   19   _____
2/23   19   3/16
8/24   19   3/16

Locust Valley Library
Locust Valley, N.Y.
11560
Tel: 516-671-1837

LV